Team Players

by Vaishali Batra

OXFORD
UNIVERSITY PRESS
AUSTRALIA & NEW ZEALAND

Team Sports

Do you play a team sport?

A sports team has two or more players. The teams play by a set of rules to **defeat** the **opposition** and win.

In a team, each player has a **role**. Whatever their role, all players compete to help their team win.

Some teams have up to 20 players.

Captains

The captain

The captain is the team's leader. The captain encourages the players to perform to the best of their ability, even in tough games.

The captain leads the team to victory in a **tournament**.

captain

The vice-captain

The vice-captain assists the captain by offering advice. The vice-captain can become the team's captain if the captain is injured or can't play.

Cricket

A cricket match is played between two teams of 11 players each. It is played on a circular ground with a strip in the middle called a pitch. The pitch has wickets at both ends. The teams take turns to score runs. The team that scores the most runs wins.

Batters

There are two batters. They stand in a safe zone in front of the wickets. They hit the ball, then run between the wickets until the ball is returned to the bowler. These runs are added to the team's score.

If a batter misses the ball and it hits the wicket, the batter is out and must leave the ground.

safe zone

If a batter hits the ball and it is caught, the batter is out.

Bowlers

The bowler's job is to bowl the ball towards the wickets. The bowler can get a batter out by hitting the wickets with the ball. Another way is to bowl so that the batter hits the ball up in the air. The batter can then be caught out.

Some bowlers spin or swing the ball so that it is hard for the batter to hit it.

Some bowlers bowl really fast.

Fielders

Fielders stand all around the ground. They help their team by stopping the batters from scoring runs. They chase the ball once the batter has hit it and return it to the bowler as quickly as possible.

The wicketkeeper stands behind the wickets and catches the ball if the batter misses it.

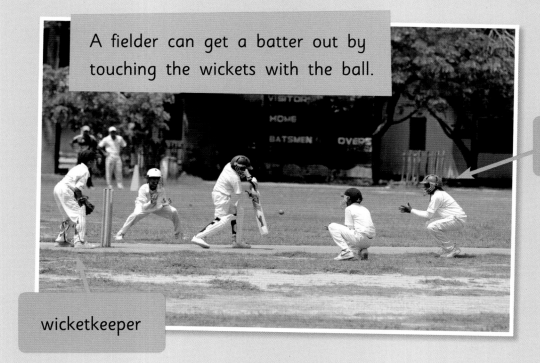

A fielder can get a batter out by touching the wickets with the ball.

fielders

wicketkeeper

Soccer

Soccer is played between two teams of 11 players each. The teams play on a rectangular field with a net at each end. The aim is to kick the ball into the net to score a goal. The team with the most goals wins the game.

Strikers

Strikers run quickly to take control of the ball and pass it to their teammates. The strikers work together to outrun the players from the other team and shoot the ball into the net.

striker

There are normally two or three strikers in a team.

Defenders

Defenders try to stop the strikers from scoring a goal. There are normally four defenders in a team. They move to outrun the attackers and take the ball from them.

defender

Defenders kick the ball far away from the opposing team's goal net.

Goalkeeper

The goalkeeper's job is to stop the opposition team strikers from scoring goals. They wear gloves and jump and dive to stop the ball from entering the net.

goalkeeper

The goalkeeper is the only player allowed to touch the ball with their hands.

Basketball

Basketball is played between two teams of five players each, on a rectangular court. Players score points by shooting the ball through high baskets (or hoops) at both ends of the court. A goal is worth one, two or three points. The team with the most points wins.

Centres

The centre's main role is to keep the opposition team players from shooting. The centres stay close to their own team's basket all through the game.

centre

Guards

There are two guards who pass the ball up, down and across the court. They can get points for their team by scoring from anywhere on the court.

When a player jumps up to force the ball down through the basket, it is called a slam dunk.

Forwards

There are two forwards in a team – a small forward and a power forward.

The small forward is active all around the court, passing the ball quickly and scoring as many points as possible.

The power forward plays close to the basket and tries to get the ball from a pass. Then the power forward moves towards the basket to shoot.

power forward

A team has just 24 seconds to shoot the ball.

Team Helpers

Some people are part of a team, but they don't actually play the game.

The coach

The coach trains the players to improve their skills. Coaches set up drills and mock games to train the team.

The coach is also responsible for choosing the players for the team and making a plan to win.

The coach's most important job is to motivate the team to play at its best.

The nutritionist

The nutritionist advises the team about health and **nutrition**. The nutritionist tells players about meals that will help them keep fit and strong, and how to make them.

breakfast

lunch

dinner

snacks

Fitness specialists

Fitness specialists help the players with strength and fitness. Some specialists help the players plan their workouts. Others teach injured players exercises to help them recover.

Fitness specialists teach players how to avoid injuries.

Team Players

Many people help a team to be successful. The players and the team helpers are all important. They all have a role to play. Are you a team player?

Glossary

to defeat: to win against a person or team

nutrition: the study of foods and how they affect our body

opposition: the person or team that you are trying to defeat

role: the job that a person has in a team

tournament: a competition that involves many teams

Index